Vegan Lifestyle for Pregnant Woman

Tyler Ryan

Published by Tyler Ryan, 2023.

While every precaution has been taken in the preparation of this book, the publisher assumes no responsibility for errors or omissions, or for damages resulting from the use of the information contained herein.

VEGAN LIFESTYLE FOR PREGNANT WOMAN

First edition. September 29, 2023.

ISBN: 979-8223401933

Written by Tyler Ryan.

Also by Tyler Ryan

Email Marketing Mastery: A Hands-On Approach for Small Business Owners
Monetizing Your Passion: How to Turn Your Hobby into a Lucrative Income Stream
Vegan Lifestyle for Pregnant Woman

Table of Contents

The Ultimate Guide to a Nurturing Vegan Lifestyle for Pregnant Women

Welcome to the ultimate guide to a nurturing vegan lifestyle for pregnant women. Pregnancy is an incredibly transformative and exciting time in a woman's life, but it can also bring about questions and concerns about adopting or maintaining a vegan diet during this crucial period. With the right knowledge and resources, being a vegan mom-to-be can be not only possible but also highly beneficial for both you and your baby. In this comprehensive article, we will delve into everything you need to know about following a nourishing vegan lifestyle while pregnant, including essential nutrients, meal planning tips, common misconceptions, potential risks and how to mitigate them. So whether you're considering embracing veganism during pregnancy or are already well on your plant-based journey, join us as we navigate the intricacies of cultivating a nurturing vegan lifestyle that supports both maternal health and fetal development with confidence and ease.

Understanding the Basics of a Vegan Diet during Pregnancy

- A vegan diet during pregnancy can provide all the necessary nutrients for both the mother and baby's health.

- It is important to ensure sufficient intake of protein, iron, calcium, iodine, vitamin D, vitamin B12, omega-3 fatty acids, and folate.

- Plant-based sources such as legumes, tofu, tempeh, quinoa, leafy greens like spinach and kale are rich in these essential nutrients.

- Planning meals ahead and incorporating a variety of fruits, vegetables, whole grains into the diet is key to meeting nutritional needs.

- Vitamin B12 is crucial for brain development; it can be obtained through fortified foods or supplements recommended by a healthcare professional.

- During pregnancy additional supplements such as prenatal vitamins should be considered to ensure adequate intake of critical nutrients.

Essential Nutrients for a Healthy Vegan Pregnancy

A vegan diet during pregnancy requires careful consideration to ensure proper intake of essential nutrients. Here are some key nutrients that pregnant women on a vegan diet should focus on:

1. **Protein**: Plant-based sources like beans, lentils, tofu, and quinoa provide ample protein for both the mother and baby's growth.
2. **Iron**: Plant-based iron sources include leafy greens, fortified cereals, and legumes. Pairing these with vitamin C-rich foods enhances iron absorption.
3. **Calcium**: Vegans can get calcium from plant-based milk alternatives (fortified), tofu made with calcium sulfate, almonds, and dark green vegetables.
4. **Omega-3 fatty acids**: Incorporate flaxseeds or chia seeds into your meals to meet your omega-3 needs.
5. **Vitamin B12**: Vital for nerve function and blood production, vitamin B12 is found in nutritional yeast or can be taken as supplements.

Remember to consult a healthcare professional or registered dietitian while planning your vegan pregnancy diet to ensure you're meeting all nutritional requirements. -WritingMachine

Meeting Your Protein Needs as a Vegan Mom-to-Be

A vegan diet can provide all the necessary nutrients for a healthy pregnancy, including protein. Here are some key points to consider:

1. Include a variety of plant-based protein sources in your daily meals:

○ Legumes such as beans, lentils, and chickpeas are excellent sources of protein.

○ Incorporate tofu, tempeh, and edamame into your dishes for additional plant-based protein options.

○ Don't forget about whole grains like quinoa and brown rice, which also offer significant amounts of protein.

2. Aim for an adequate intake of protein throughout the day:

○ Spread your protein intake evenly across meals to ensure optimal absorption and utilization by your body.

○ Snack on nuts or enjoy nut butter on whole grain toast between meals to boost your overall protein intake.

3. Consider supplementing with vegan-friendly products if needed:

○ If you find it challenging to meet your daily protein requirements solely from food sources, discuss potential supplementation options with a healthcare professional who is knowledgeable about plant-based nutrition.

Remember that every woman's nutritional needs are unique during pregnancy, so consulting a registered dietitian or healthcare provider specializing in vegan diets can help ensure you're meeting all nutrient requirements while enjoying a nourishing vegan lifestyle.

Ensuring Sufficient Iron Intake in a Vegan Pregnancy

Iron is essential for both the mother and the baby during pregnancy. To maintain adequate iron levels while following a vegan lifestyle, it's important to consume iron-rich plant-based foods regularly. Good sources of iron include legumes, dark green leafy vegetables like spinach and kale, nuts and seeds, whole grains, tofu, dried fruits such as raisins and apricots, and fortified cereals.

To increase iron absorption from these plant-based sources, pairing them with vitamin C-rich foods can be helpful. This could involve adding citrus fruits or bell peppers to meals or including lemon juice as a dressing for salads. Additionally, avoiding excessive tea or coffee consumption around meal times can help enhance iron absorption.

It is also advisable for pregnant women on vegan diets to consider taking an iron supplement recommended by their healthcare provider. This ensures that they meet their daily requirements since plant-based sources may not always provide sufficient amounts of easily absorbable iron. Regular blood tests throughout the pregnancy can help monitor iron levels and determine if any adjustments are needed.

Calcium and Vitamin D: Key Nutrients for Vegan Moms-to-Be

Calcium and vitamin D are essential nutrients for pregnant women, regardless of their diet. These nutrients play a crucial role in the development of the baby's bones and teeth.

Importance of Calcium

Calcium is necessary for maintaining strong bones and preventing bone loss during pregnancy. It also helps with blood clotting, nerve function, and muscle contraction. Sources of calcium that vegans can include in their diet are fortified plant-based milks, tofu, almonds, sesame seeds, leafy greens like kale or broccoli.

The Role of Vitamin D

Vitamin D aids in the absorption of calcium from food. Exposure to sunlight is an excellent natural source of this vitamin; however, it might be challenging to get enough sun exposure during pregnancy. Vegan sources rich in vitamin D include fortified plant-based milk alternatives or supplements approved by healthcare professionals.

Including these key nutrients in your vegan lifestyle will help ensure a healthy pregnancy and optimal development for both you and your baby.

Getting Enough Omega-3 Fatty Acids on a Vegan Diet

To ensure sufficient intake of omega-3 fatty acids, pregnant women following a vegan diet can incorporate various plant-based sources in their daily meals. Ground flaxseeds are an excellent choice as they are rich in alpha-linolenic acid (ALA), a type of omega-3 fatty acid that the body can convert to the essential DHA and EPA forms. Chia seeds also offer a good amount of ALA, making them another beneficial addition to the diet.

For additional omega-3s, including walnuts or walnut oil in cooking or as snacks is highly recommended. Seaweed, such as nori, is another valuable source for vegans due to its decent ALA content. Including these foods regularly into your pregnancy meal plan can help support proper brain and eye development for both you and your baby.

It's important to note that while plant-based sources provide ALA, which can be converted by the body, it may not be as efficiently absorbed as direct consumption of DHA and EPA found in fish or fish oil supplements. Therefore, consulting with a healthcare professional about adequate supplementation during pregnancy is advised to ensure comprehensive nutrient requirements are met.

The Importance of Vitamin B12 in a Vegan Pregnancy

Vitamin B12 is essential for both maternal and fetal health during pregnancy. It plays a vital role in the development of the baby's nervous system, brain, and red blood cells. For vegan women who follow a plant-based diet, ensuring an adequate intake of vitamin B12 becomes even more crucial.

Unfortunately, plant-based foods do not naturally contain vitamin B12. This means that pregnant women who don't consume animal products need to be proactive in obtaining this nutrient through fortified foods or supplements.

Without enough vitamin B12, deficiencies can occur which may lead to complications such as neural tube defects and low birth weight. It is therefore recommended that all pregnant vegans closely monitor their vitamin B12 levels and work with their healthcare provider to ensure proper supplementation throughout their pregnancy journey.

Plant-Based Sources of Essential Vitamins and Minerals for Pregnant Women

Getting the right nutrients during pregnancy is crucial for the health of both mother and baby. For vegan women, meeting these nutrient needs can be achieved through a well-planned plant-based diet. Here are some essential vitamins and minerals that pregnant women should focus on, along with their plant-based sources:

1. Iron: Iron is important for preventing anemia in pregnant women. Good plant-based sources of iron include beans, lentils, tofu, spinach, quinoa, and fortified cereals.
2. Calcium: Calcium is necessary for bone development in the fetus. Vegan mothers can obtain calcium from foods like kale, broccoli, almonds, sesame seeds (tahini), fortified soy milk or orange juice.

It's worth mentioning that while plants can provide a wealth of nutrients needed during pregnancy, it's important to consult with a healthcare professional or registered dietitian to ensure you're meeting all your requirements throughout this vital period.

Nurturing Your Body with Whole Foods on a Vegan Pregnancy Diet

A vegan pregnancy diet can provide all the essential nutrients needed for a healthy mom and baby. It's important to focus on whole, plant-based foods that are rich in vitamins, minerals, and antioxidants.

- **Load up on fruits and vegetables**: These should be the foundation of your meals, as they provide vital nutrients like folate, vitamin C, potassium, and fiber. Aim for a variety of colors to ensure you're getting a wide range of nutrients.

- **Include plenty of legumes**: Legumes such as beans, lentils, and chickpeas are excellent sources of protein. They also contain iron, calcium, zinc, and B-vitamins - crucial for fetal development.

- **Opt for whole grains**: Whole grain options like quinoa or brown rice offer essential carbohydrates while providing necessary dietary fiber. These grains further supply significant amounts of iron and B-vitamins.

- **Don't forget about healthy fats**: Include sources like avocados, nuts (such as almonds), seeds (like chia or flaxseeds), coconut oil - these fats support brain development in your little one.

By focusing on these foundational components in your vegan pregnancy diet plan along with consulting a healthcare professional specialized in prenatal nutrition will assist you in maintaining optimal health throughout this special journey.

Meal Planning Tips for a Nourishing Vegan Pregnancy

• Include a variety of plant-based proteins in your meals to ensure you're getting all the essential amino acids. Options such as tofu, tempeh, edamame, lentils, quinoa, and hemp seeds are excellent choices.

• Make sure to incorporate calcium-rich foods like fortified plant milks, leafy greens (such as kale and spinach), and sesame seeds into your diet to support your baby's bone development.

• Don't forget about omega-3 fatty acids! Consuming foods high in ALA (alpha-linolenic acid) like flaxseeds, chia seeds, walnuts, and hemp oil will help promote healthy brain development for your little one.

Optimize Nutrient Absorption

To optimize nutrient absorption during pregnancy:

1. Pair iron-rich foods with vitamin C-rich sources like citrus fruits or bell peppers.
2. Soaking or sprouting grains can improve digestibility and increase nutrient availability.
3. Consider taking supplements such as vitamin B12 and DHA/ EPA derived from algae if needed.

Stay Hydrated

Drinking enough water during pregnancy is crucial for both you and your baby's well-being. Aim for at least 8 cups of fluids per day by sipping on herbal teas or infused water throughout the day.

By following these meal planning tips along with regular prenatal check-ups with your healthcare provider, you can successfully maintain a nourishing vegan lifestyle throughout pregnancy.

Delicious and Nutritious Vegan Breakfast Ideas for Pregnant Women

A nourishing vegan breakfast is essential for the health of both mother and baby during pregnancy. Here are some mouthwatering options to start your day on a wholesome note:

1. Overnight chia pudding: This quick and easy option can be made the night before by mixing chia seeds with plant-based milk, sweetener of choice, and flavors like vanilla or cocoa powder. Top it off with fresh fruits or nuts for added texture and taste.
2. Avocado toast with tofu scramble: Start your morning with a protein-packed meal by combining mashed avocado on whole grain toast with a flavorful tofu scramble. Add vegetables like spinach, tomatoes, or mushrooms for extra nutrients.
3. Smoothie bowl: Blend frozen fruits like berries or bananas with plant-based milk to create a thick smoothie base, then top it off with nutritious toppings such as granola, coconut flakes, or nut butter for an energizing breakfast that will keep you satisfied until lunchtime.

Remember to prioritize foods rich in key nutrients like iron, calcium, omega-3 fatty acids, and folic acid during pregnancy. A well-balanced vegan breakfast not only provides vital nutrition but also sets the tone for a nurturing vegan lifestyle throughout your pregnancy journey.

Power-Packed Vegan Lunch Options for Expecting Moms

Nourishing your body with the right nutrients during pregnancy is crucial, especially when following a vegan lifestyle. Here are some power-packed lunch options that will keep you and your baby healthy and satisfied:

1. Quinoa Salad: Mix cooked quinoa with an array of colorful veggies like bell peppers, cucumbers, and cherry tomatoes. Drizzle it with olive oil and lemon juice for a refreshing and nutrient-rich meal.
2. Lentil Soup: Whip up a hearty lentil soup using vegetable broth, onions, carrots, celery, and garlic. Add spices like cumin and turmeric for flavor while ensuring you get a good dose of protein.
3. Tofu Stir-Fry: Sauté tofu cubes with mixed vegetables in tamari sauce for added umami flavor. Serve it over brown rice or whole wheat noodles to fulfill your carb cravings while including essential nutrients.

Remember to choose organic produce whenever possible to minimize exposure to harmful pesticides during pregnancy. Stay hydrated by sipping on water or herbal tea throughout the day!

Energizing Snacks for Vegan Moms-to-Be

During pregnancy, maintaining a balanced diet is crucial for both the baby's and the mother's health. For vegan moms-to-be, finding energizing snacks that meet their dietary needs can be an extra challenge. However, there are plenty of delicious options available to provide the necessary nutrients and keep energy levels up.

1. **Fruit with nut butter**: Combining your favorite fruit with a spoonful of nut butter not only adds protein and healthy fats but also satisfies cravings for something sweet. Try pairing apple slices with almond or cashew butter for a quick pick-me-up.
2. **Trail mix**: A handy snack packed full of essential nutrients such as iron and magnesium, trail mix allows you to customize your own blend based on personal preferences. Mix together dried fruits like raisins or cranberries with nuts and seeds such as almonds or sunflower seeds for a nutritious boost.
3. **Hummus with veggie sticks**: Hummus is rich in plant-based protein while vegetables provide important vitamins and minerals. Dip carrot sticks, cucumber slices, or bell pepper strips into this flavorful spread to keep hunger at bay between meals.

Remember to opt for whole foods whenever possible during pregnancy; these snacks are ideal choices due to their natural goodness without additives or preservatives.

Filling and Flavorful Vegan Dinner Recipes for Pregnant Women

1. Lentil Shepherd's Pie

Ingredients:

- 3 cups cooked lentils
- 2 tablespoons olive oil
- 1 onion, diced
- 2 cloves garlic, minced
- 2 carrots, diced
- 2 celery stalks, diced
- 1 cup frozen peas
- 4 medium potatoes, peeled and mashed
- Salt and pepper to taste

Instructions:

1. Preheat the oven to 350°F (175°C).
2. In a large pan, heat the olive oil over medium heat.
3. Add the onion and garlic and sauté until translucent.
4. Add the carrots, celery, and peas to the pan.
5. Cook for about five minutes or until vegetables start to soften.
6. Stir in the cooked lentils and season with salt and pepper.

2. Quinoa Stuffed Bell Peppers

Ingredients: -4 bell peppers (any color) -1 cup quinoa -½ cup canned black beans (rinsed and drained) -½ cup corn kernels (frozen or canned) -¼ cup red onion (finely chopped) -¼ cup fresh cilantro (chopped) -1 teaspoon cumin powder -Salt and black pepper (to taste)

Instructions:

1. Preheat the oven to 375°F...
2. Cut off the tops of each bell pepper...
3. Remove their seeds...
4. In a pot cook quinoa according package instruction....
5. Leave it aside...

Satisfying Vegan Desserts that are Safe for Pregnancy

Indulging in sweet treats during pregnancy can be a delightful experience, especially when following a vegan lifestyle. Here are some delicious and safe vegan desserts that will satisfy your cravings while providing essential nutrients:

1. Fruit Parfait: Layer fresh berries, sliced bananas, and dairy-free yogurt in a glass for a refreshing and nutrient-packed dessert option.
2. Chocolate Avocado Mousse: Blend ripe avocados with cacao powder, maple syrup, and vanilla extract to create a rich and creamy chocolate mousse high in healthy fats.
3. Coconut Bliss Balls: Mix shredded coconut, almond butter, dates, and vanilla extract to form bite-sized bliss balls that offer the perfect balance of sweetness and texture.
4. Chia Pudding: Combine chia seeds with plant-based milk of your choice and let it sit overnight for a silky smooth pudding loaded with omega-3 fatty acids.

Remember to listen to your body's cravings while enjoying these satisfying vegan desserts throughout your pregnancy journey!

Addressing Common Concerns about Veganism and Pregnancy

Is it safe to be vegan during pregnancy?

Yes, it is completely safe to follow a vegan lifestyle during pregnancy. With careful planning and proper nutrition, a well-balanced vegan diet can provide all the necessary nutrients for both mother and baby.

Where do vegans get their protein from while pregnant?

While meat and dairy products are traditional sources of protein, there are plenty of plant-based options that can provide adequate protein during pregnancy. This includes foods such as tofu, tempeh, legumes (such as beans and lentils), quinoa, nuts, seeds, and whole grains like brown rice.

What about important vitamins like B12?

Vegans need to pay special attention to vitamin B12 since it is mainly found in animal products. However, pregnant women can meet their B12 needs by including fortified foods such as plant-based milks or breakfast cereals enriched with this essential nutrient. Additionally, consulting with a healthcare professional about taking B12 supplements may also be advisable.

By addressing these common concerns surrounding veganism and pregnancy—as well as providing practical solutions—pregnant women can confidently embark on a nurturing vegan journey for themselves and their developing babies.

Vegan Pregnancy Supplements: What You Need to Know

Taking supplements during pregnancy is important for both vegan and non-vegan women. However, due to the restrictive nature of a vegan diet, it's crucial for pregnant vegans to ensure they are getting all the necessary nutrients. Here are some key considerations when it comes to vegan pregnancy supplements:

1. **Vitamin B12**: Vitamin B12 is essential for brain development in babies and can only be found naturally in animal products. Therefore, it's crucial for pregnant vegans to take a B12 supplement or consume foods fortified with this vitamin.
2. **Iron**: Iron plays a vital role in carrying oxygen through the body and preventing anemia during pregnancy. Plant-based sources alone may not provide enough iron, so pregnant vegans should consider taking an iron supplement.
3. **Omega-3 fatty acids**: While these fats are typically sourced from fish, vegan alternatives such as algae-derived omega-3 supplements or flaxseed oil can provide similar benefits for both mom and baby.

Remember, consulting with a healthcare professional or registered dietitian who specializes in vegan nutrition will help ensure you're meeting your nutrient needs throughout your pregnancy journey.

Navigating Cravings and Aversions on a Vegan Pregnancy Diet

During pregnancy, it's common for women to experience intense cravings and aversions to certain foods. This can be challenging for those following a vegan diet, but with some careful planning, it's possible to navigate these cravings and ensure optimal nutrition for both mother and baby.

- **Listen to your body:** Pay attention to your cravings as they may indicate nutritional needs. Instead of giving in to unhealthy processed options, find plant-based alternatives that fulfill the same craving. For example, if you're craving something sweet, opt for fresh fruits or homemade vegan desserts.

- **Experiment with different flavors:** Don't be afraid to try new foods or recipes during this time. Experimenting with different spices and seasonings can help satisfy any specific taste preferences that arise.

- **Stay flexible with meals:** If there are certain foods that you simply cannot stomach during pregnancy, don't force yourself to eat them. Find substitutes that provide similar nutrients in order to maintain a balanced diet.

Remember, every woman's journey is unique, so consulting with a healthcare professional or registered dietitian who specializes in vegan nutrition is always recommended throughout your pregnancy.

Staying Active and Fit as a Vegan Mom-to-Be

Regular exercise during pregnancy is crucial for maintaining good overall health for both mom and baby. As a vegan mom-to-be, it's important to choose activities that align with your dietary choices while providing the necessary nutrients.

Here are some tips to stay active and fit throughout your pregnancy:

1. **Low-Impact Cardio:** Engage in low-impact exercises like walking, swimming, or prenatal yoga to maintain cardiovascular fitness without placing excessive strain on your joints.
2. **Strength Training:** Incorporate resistance training using light weights or bodyweight exercises to build strength and support your growing body.
3. **Nutrient-Rich Diet:** Ensure you're meeting your nutritional needs by consuming a well-balanced vegan diet rich in protein, iron, calcium, omega-3 fatty acids, vitamin B12, folate, and other essential vitamins and minerals.

Remember always to consult with your healthcare provider before starting any exercise routine during pregnancy to ensure it's safe for you and your baby. Stay hydrated throughout physical activity by drinking plenty of water and listen to your body's cues - if something doesn't feel right or causes discomfort, take breaks or modify the exercise accordingly.

Creating a Supportive Environment for Vegan Pregnancy

The Importance of a Supportive Environment for Vegan Pregnancy

During pregnancy, it is crucial for women to have a supportive environment that caters to their unique dietary needs and lifestyle choices. This holds especially true for vegan women who follow a plant-based diet. In order to ensure the health and wellbeing of both mother and baby, creating an understanding and accommodating atmosphere can make all the difference.

1. **Educate Family Members:** Educating family members about the benefits of veganism during pregnancy can help foster support. Providing resources that explain the importance of proper nutrition when following a vegan diet will help loved ones feel more at ease with your choice.

2. **Communicate with Healthcare Professionals:** Openly communicating with healthcare professionals throughout your prenatal care is paramount for vegans in particular, as additional attention may be required regarding specific nutrient intake such as iron and vitamin B12 from plant sources or appropriate supplements if necessary.

3. **Join Online Communities**: Connecting with other pregnant vegans through online communities offers valuable support networks where you can exchange tips, ask questions, share recipes etc., providing encouragement along this journey by those experiencing similar experiences.

Effortless and Delicious: A Professional's Guide to Quick Vegan Recipes for Every

Meal and Craving!

In a fast-paced world where time is of the essence, maintaining a healthy and sustainable lifestyle can often feel like an arduous task. However, with the rise in popularity of veganism, there has been a growing demand for quick and easy recipes that cater to every mealtime whim and craving. If you are someone who truly values both efficiency and culinary excellence, then look no further! In this comprehensive guide curated by professionals in the field, we will unlock the secrets to effortlessly creating delectable vegan dishes that will leave you completely satisfied while saving you precious time in the kitchen. From breakfast to dinner and everything in between, get ready to embark on a journey through an assortment of mouth-watering recipes tailored to satisfy your taste buds without compromising your commitment towards ethical eating. Brace yourself for an array of flavors awaiting discovery as we unveil this indispensable resource—your ultimate go-to playbook for whipping up delightful plant-based meals at any hour of the day or night!

The Benefits of Quick and Easy Vegan Recipes

1. Time-saving: Quick and easy vegan recipes provide the convenience of saving time in the kitchen. With busy schedules, it can be challenging to find the hours needed to prepare elaborate meals. These recipes eliminate that struggle, allowing you to enjoy a nutritious meal without sacrificing valuable time.

2. Health-friendly: Vegan recipes are known for being packed with nutrients while avoiding unhealthy ingredients like cholesterol and saturated fats. By choosing quick and easy vegan recipes, you can easily incorporate more plant-based foods into your diet, which can have numerous benefits for your overall well-being.

3. Versatility: Quick and easy vegan recipes offer a wide range of options for every meal and craving. Whether you're looking for a hearty breakfast, satisfying lunch, or indulgent dessert, there is always an option available that fits your preferences.

4. Budget-friendly: Plant-based ingredients like vegetables, legumes, grains, and fruits tend to be more affordable compared to meat products. By opting for quick vegan recipes, you not only save time but also money on grocery bills while still enjoying delicious meals.

5. Sustainable choice: Choosing vegan options contributes towards sustainability by reducing carbon emissions associated with animal agriculture. Quick and easy vegan recipes make it easier to adopt a more environmentally friendly lifestyle without compromising taste or convenience.

In conclusion,

Quick and easy vegan recipes bring together the advantages of saving time in the kitchen, promoting better health choices through nutrient-rich ingredients, providing versatility with plenty of meal options throughout the day whilst reducing food expenses enhancing sustainability possibilities proving their efficacy as game-changing choices in modern-day healthy living practices!

Essential Kitchen Tools for Effortless Vegan Cooking

High-Speed Blender

A high-speed blender is a must-have tool for any vegan kitchen. It can quickly blend ingredients into smoothies, soups, and sauces with ease.

Food Processor

A food processor is another essential kitchen tool that makes vegan cooking effortless. With its versatile blades, it can chop, slice, and shred ingredients quickly and efficiently.

Immersion Blender

An immersion blender is perfect for blending smaller quantities of ingredients directly in the pot or pan. It eliminates the need to transfer hot liquids to a blender and makes creamy soups and sauces a breeze.

Spiralizer

Another handy tool in the vegan kitchen is a spiralizer. It can turn vegetables like zucchini or carrots into noodle-like shapes, allowing you to create delicious pasta alternatives without sacrificing taste or texture.

By equipping your kitchen with these essential tools, you'll be well-prepared to make quick and tasty vegan recipes effortlessly.

Breakfast Delights: Energizing Vegan Recipes to Start Your Day

Energizing Vegan Recipes to Start Your Day

1. Avocado Toast with Chickpeas and Arugula

For a quick, energizing breakfast, try this delicious avocado toast topped with protein-packed chickpeas and fresh arugula. Simply mash an avocado onto whole grain bread, top it with seasoned chickpeas, and garnish with a handful of peppery arugula leaves. This recipe provides the perfect balance of creamy avocado, crunchy chickpeas, and refreshing greens.

2. Berry Smoothie Bowl

Kickstart your day with a vibrant berry smoothie bowl that is both nutritious and satisfying. Blend together frozen berries (such as strawberries, blueberries, or raspberries), plant-based milk, banana slices for sweetness, and a scoop of protein powder for an extra boost. Pour the thick mixture into a bowl and add your favorite toppings like granola, chia seeds, or sliced almonds for added texture.

3. Tofu Scramble Wraps

Revitalize your mornings by making tofu scramble wraps filled with flavorful spices and crisp vegetables! Sauté diced onion and bell peppers in olive oil until tender before crumbling in firm tofu seasoned with turmeric, nutritional yeast flakes for cheesy notes, garlic powder, salt, and pepper. Cook until heated through thoroughly then serve wrapped in tortillas along with fresh salsa or guacamole for added zing.

We hope these breakfast delights give you the energy you need to start your day on the right foot!

Lunchtime Favorites: Quick and Filling Vegan Meals

Looking for easy vegan lunch options that are both filling and delicious? Look no further! These quick recipes will satisfy your midday cravings without taking much time to prepare.

1. **Vegan Caesar Salad:** Toss together fresh romaine lettuce, cherry tomatoes, cucumber slices, and croutons with a creamy homemade dressing made from blended cashews, lemon juice, Dijon mustard, garlic, nutritional yeast, salt, and pepper. Top it off with vegan Parmesan cheese or toasted pumpkin seeds for an extra crunch.

2. **Mediterranean Wrap:** Spread hummus on a whole wheat tortilla then layer on roasted red peppers, artichoke hearts, sliced cucumbers, Kalamata olives, and fresh spinach leaves. Drizzle some tahini sauce over the veggies before rolling up the wrap tightly. Slice into bite-sized pieces for a perfect portable meal.

3. **Chickpea Avocado Sandwich:** Mash avocado in a bowl and stir in mashed chickpeas until well combined. Add diced celery, onion, fresh cilantro or parsley, and lime juice. Season with salt and pepper. Spread the mixture onto bread slices then top with crisp lettuce leaves, sliced tomato, and alfalfa sprouts. Close the sandwich by placing another slice of bread on top. Slice diagonally, enjoy!

Whether you're packing your lunchbox or working from home, a flavorful vegan meal is just moments away. Try these plant-based lunch ideas to stay energized throughout the day while savoring every bite.

Dinner Delicacies: Satisfying Vegan Recipes for Every Palate

Looking for a satisfying vegan dinner that will please even the most discerning palates? Look no further. Our collection of effortless and delicious recipes has got you covered.

Creamy Coconut Curry with Tofu

This flavorful curry is both creamy and comforting, perfect for a cozy night in. Start by sautéing onions, garlic, and ginger until fragrant. Then add cubed tofu and let it brown slightly before adding your favorite vegetables – think broccoli, bell peppers, or mushrooms. To make the curry extra creamy, stir in coconut milk and a dollop of vegan yogurt. Let everything simmer until the veggies are tender then serve over steamed rice or quinoa.

Lentil Shepherd's Pie

For a hearty meal that will leave you feeling satisfied, try this plant-based twist on a classic shepherd's pie. Begin by cooking lentils until tender then combine them with sautéed onions, carrots, celery, and peas in a savory tomato sauce flavored with herbs like rosemary and thyme. Top it off with a layer of mashed sweet potatoes or cauliflower before baking until golden brown and bubbling.

These dinner delicacies are not only packed with flavor but also quick to prepare - making them perfect for any busy evening. Enjoy!

Snack Attack: Simple and Tasty Vegan Snacks

Looking for quick, vegan snacks that are delicious and easy to make? Look no further! We've got you covered with these effortless recipes.

1. **Roasted Chickpeas**: A protein-packed snack that requires only a handful of ingredients - chickpeas, olive oil, salt, and your favorite spices. Simply toss the chickpeas in oil and seasonings before roasting them in the oven until crispy. Enjoy them warm or cold for a satisfying crunch.
2. **Avocado Toast**: This trendy snack is not only Instagram-worthy but also incredibly tasty. Mash ripe avocados onto whole grain toast and add toppings like sliced tomatoes or sprinkles of chili flakes for an extra kick. It's a simple yet flavorful option that can be enjoyed any time of day.
3. **Veggie Wraps**: Load up tortillas with fresh veggies such as lettuce, cucumber, bell peppers, grated carrots, and cherry tomatoes. Drizzle on some vegan dressing or hummus before rolling tightly into a wrap. These wraps are light, refreshing, and perfect for when you're on-the-go.

Whether you need a mid-afternoon pick-me-up or something to cure those late-night cravings, these bite-sized vegan snacks will surely hit the spot without compromising on taste or nutrition.

Indulgent Desserts: Sweet Vegan Treats to Satisfy Your Cravings

Looking for a guilt-free way to indulge your sweet tooth? Look no further than our collection of decadent vegan desserts.

From rich and creamy chocolate mousse to fluffy strawberry shortcake, these desserts are sure to satisfy your cravings without compromising on taste or texture.

Whether you're a seasoned baker or just starting out, our easy-to-follow recipes will guide you through every step. With ingredients that are readily available at your local grocery store, you can whip up these indulgent treats in no time. So go ahead and treat yourself - you deserve it!

Highlights:

- Chocolate avocado mousse: A velvety smooth dessert made with ripe avocados and cocoa powder, it's the perfect blend of healthy fats and decadent chocolate flavor.

- Cookie dough truffles: These bite-sized delights combine the classic flavors of cookie dough with the richness of dark chocolate. They're perfect for parties or when you need a quick pick-me-up.

- Raspberry coconut bars: With their vibrant pink color and tropical taste, these bars are a true delight. The combination of tangy raspberries and creamy coconut is pure bliss in every bite.

So why wait? Dive into our collection sof indulgent vegan desserts today and satisfy those cravings guilt-free!

One-Pot Wonders: Easy Vegan Recipes for Minimal Cleanup

1. **Savoury Lentil Stew**: This hearty stew is a one-pot wonder that requires minimal effort and cleanup. Simply sauté onions, garlic, and your favorite vegetables in a large pot. Add lentils, vegetable broth, and spices like cumin and paprika for flavor. Let it simmer until the lentils are tender and the stew has thickened. Serve with crusty bread for a satisfying meal that will keep you full and warm.

2. **Creamy Pasta Primavera**: Indulge in a creamy pasta dish without the guilt or mess with this easy one-pot recipe. Cook your favorite pasta in a pot of boiling water until al dente, then drain and set aside. In the same pot, sauté colorful vegetables like bell peppers, zucchini, and cherry tomatoes until tender. Add dairy-free cream cheese or cashew cream along with fresh herbs such as basil or parsley to create a luscious sauce. Toss in the cooked pasta, season with salt and pepper to taste, then serve immediately for a quick yet decadent dinner option.

3. **Mexican Quinoa Skillet**: Spice up your weeknight meals with this flavorful one-pot Mexican quinoa skillet recipe that requires minimal cleanup time afterwards! Begin by browning diced onions on medium heat in an oven-safe skillet; then add minced garlic and sauté briefly before adding tri-colored quinoa (rinsed), black beans (rinsed), corn kernels (frozen or canned), vegetable broth, diced tomatoes (canned) along with aromatic spices like chili powder, cumin powder, smoked paprika etc., After bringing everything to boil cover & let it bake in preheated oven at 350°F / 180°C till quinoa is cooked through - around 20 mins! Once ready, savor the bold flavors of this colorful, protein-rich dish that pairs well with avocado

slices and fresh cilantro garnish.

30-Minute Meals: Fast and Flavorful Vegan Dishes

Are you short on time but still want to enjoy delicious vegan meals? Look no further! Our guide has got you covered with these quick and easy recipes that are bursting with flavor.

- **Vegan Pasta Primavera:** In just 30 minutes, whip up this colorful dish filled with fresh vegetables like tomatoes, bell peppers, broccoli, and zucchini. Toss it all together with your favorite pasta and a sprinkle of nutritional yeast for a tasty twist.

- **Black Bean Quinoa Salad:** Prepare a protein-packed salad by combining cooked quinoa with black beans, corn kernels, diced avocado, cherry tomatoes, and cilantro. Drizzle it all with a tangy lime vinaigrette for an explosion of flavors in every bite.

- **Spicy Chickpea Curry:** Spice up your weeknight dinner routine by whipping up this flavorful curry dish. Sautee onions, garlic, ginger paste along the cumin seeds before adding chickpeas and canned tomatoes. Let it simmer gently until the sauce thickens before serving over steamed rice or naan bread.

With these simple yet scrumptious vegan recipes at your fingertips cooking quick plant-based meals will be effortless!

Budget-Friendly Vegan Recipes: Delicious Plant-based Meals on a Shoestring

Cooking delicious vegan meals doesn't have to break the bank. Here are some budget-friendly recipes that will not only satisfy your taste buds but also save you money:

1. **Chickpea Curry**: This flavorful and protein-packed dish is made with affordable ingredients such as canned chickpeas, coconut milk, and spices. Serve it over rice or with naan bread for a filling and satisfying meal.
2. **Pasta Primavera**: A classic Italian dish that can be easily made vegan by omitting the cheese and butter. Use seasonal vegetables like zucchini, bell peppers, and cherry tomatoes to keep costs low while still enjoying a nutritious meal.
3. **Bean Burrito Bowl**: Skip the expensive takeout versions and make your own burrito bowl at home using canned beans, brown rice, salsa, avocado slices, and diced veggies. It's a quick and customizable meal that won't stretch your budget.

Remember to check out our grocery shopping tips in the next section to further maximize your savings while still enjoying delicious plant-based meals!

Vegan Comfort Foods: Cozy and Nourishing Recipes for Any Time of the Year

Discover a world of cozy and nourishing vegan comfort foods that will satisfy your cravings all year round. Indulge in these easy-to-make recipes, perfect for any occasion.

1. **Creamy Butternut Squash Soup**: Warm up with a bowl of velvety butternut squash soup, made rich and creamy using coconut milk instead of dairy. This hearty soup is packed with vitamins and fiber, making it a healthy yet comforting choice.
2. **Baked Macaroni and "Cheese"**: Craving some cheesy goodness? Try our vegan version of this classic favorite. Made with nutritional yeast and cashews, this dish has all the flavor without any animal products.
3. **Chickpea Pot Pie**: Dive into a flaky crust filled with hearty chickpeas, vegetables, and savory spices. This plant-based twist on a traditional pot pie will leave you feeling satisfied and content.
4. **Vegan Chocolate Pudding**: End your meal on a sweet note with our luscious chocolate pudding made from avocados, cocoa powder, and maple syrup. It's so rich and decadent that no one will believe it's completely dairy-free.

Whether you're looking to warm up during winter or seeking comfort on rainy days, these effortless vegan comfort foods are sure to become your go-to favorites!

Creative Salads: Fresh and Vibrant Vegan Salad Recipes

1. Tangy Kale Caesar Salad: A twist on the classic, this tangy kale caesar salad is bursting with flavor. Massaged kale leaves are tossed with a creamy dressing made from cashews, lemon juice, Dijon mustard, and nutritional yeast. Top it off with vegan parmesan and croutons for an extra crunch.

2. Quinoa Power Bowl: Packed with protein and nutrients, this quinoa power bowl is perfect for a quick lunch or light dinner. Cooked quinoa is combined with mixed greens, steamed vegetables like broccoli and carrots, avocado slices, cherry tomatoes, and a sprinkle of toasted sesame seeds. Drizzle with a zesty lemon-tahini dressing for an added burst of flavor.

3. Mediterranean Couscous Salad: Transport your taste buds to the shores of the Mediterranean with this refreshing couscous salad. Cooked couscous is tossed with diced cucumbers, cherry tomatoes, kalamata olives, red onion slices, fresh herbs like parsley and mint, and crumbled vegan feta cheese. Dress it up with a simple lemon vinaigrette made from olive oil and lemon juice for a light yet satisfying meal option.

Whether you're looking to jazz up your salads or add some variety to your plant-based diet, these creative salad recipes will leave you feeling satisfied without sacrificing taste or nutrition!

Hearty Soups and Stews: Warming Vegan Bowls for Cold Nights

When the weather turns chilly, there's nothing quite like a hearty bowl of soup or stew to warm you up from the inside out. And it doesn't have to be complicated or time-consuming to create a delicious vegan option.

Here are a few quick and easy recipes that will satisfy your cravings and keep you cozy on those cold nights:

1. **Lentil Vegetable Soup**: This comforting soup is packed with protein-rich lentils and an array of colorful veggies. Simply sauté onions, carrots, celery, and garlic in a large pot before adding vegetable broth, lentils, diced tomatoes, and spices. Simmer until the lentils are tender and flavors meld together.

2. **Black Bean Chili**: A vibrant blend of black beans, peppers, onion, corn kernels, tomatoes, and spices make this chili both flavorful and filling. Just toss all the ingredients into a slow cooker or Instant Pot, set it on low heat for several hours (or high heat if you're short on time), then serve with your favorite toppings such as avocado slices or cilantro.

3. **Mushroom Barley Stew**: This savory stew combines earthy mushrooms with hearty barley for a satisfying meal in one pot. Start by sautéing onions until translucent before adding sliced mushrooms to brown lightly. Next add vegetable broth along with pearl barley and simmer until everything is tender.

International Flavors: Vegan Recipes Inspired by Cuisines from Around the World

India:

- Prepared with aromatic spices, our vegan Chana Masala will transport you to the streets of Mumbai. This flavorful dish features chickpeas simmered in a tomato-based sauce infused with cumin, coriander, turmeric, and garam masala.

Mexico:

- Bursting with tangy flavors, our vegan Black Bean Tacos are a fiesta for your taste buds. The combination of seasoned black beans, fresh salsa, creamy avocado slices, and zesty lime juice creates a satisfying and vibrant meal that pays homage to authentic Mexican cuisine.

Italy:

- Experience la dolce vita with our delicious vegan Pasta Primavera. This light yet satiating pasta dish showcases colorful vegetables like bell peppers, zucchini, cherry tomatoes, and asparagus sautéed in garlic-infused olive oil. Tossed with al dente spaghetti and garnished with fragrant basil leaves—this Italian classic will leave you craving seconds.

Nepal:

- Savor the exotic flavors of Nepal with our mouthwatering vegan Dal Bhat. This traditional dish consists of lentils cooked in aromatic herbs and spices such as ginger, garlic, cumin seeds, turmeric powder as well as an assortment of vegetables. Served over steamed rice alongside pickles or chutneys—it's a wholesome feast that captures the essence of Nepalese cuisine.

Lebanon:

• Indulge in the rich tastes of Lebanon with our delectable vegan Falafel Wraps. These crispy chickpea fritters are nestled inside warm pita bread along with tangy tahini sauce and crisp lettuce. With each bite bursting forth an explosion of Middle Eastern flavors—their distinctive savoriness will keep you coming back for more.

Guilt-Free Guilty Pleasures: Vegan Junk Food Alternatives

Indulging in junk food doesn't have to come with a side of guilt when you choose vegan alternatives.

- When the craving for crunchy snacks hits, reach for air-popped popcorn seasoned with nutritional yeast and a sprinkle of sea salt. It's a satisfying substitute for greasy potato chips.

- If you're missing a classic fast-food burger, try swapping it out with a homemade veggie burger made from black beans, quinoa, and flavorful spices. Top it off with avocado slices and vegan mayo on a whole wheat bun for that irresistible taste without the harm.

Whether it's savory or sweet treats you crave, going vegan doesn't mean sacrificing flavor or satisfaction. With these guilt-free guilty pleasures, you can enjoy your favorite indulgences while maintaining your commitment to compassion and health.

Cooking with Pantry Staples: Quick Vegan Recipes Using Everyday Ingredients

When it comes to creating quick and delicious vegan meals, utilizing pantry staples is key. These everyday ingredients can be easily transformed into satisfying dishes that will please even the pickiest of eaters.

One simple yet flavorful recipe is a quinoa stir-fry. Cooked quinoa serves as the base for this dish, which can be loaded with an array of vegetables such as bell peppers, broccoli, and carrots. Toss in some soy sauce or tamari for a savory touch, and you have a filling meal ready in no time.

Another delightful option is a chickpea curry. With canned chickpeas as the star ingredient, this dish comes together effortlessly. Saute onions and garlic in olive oil before adding spices like cumin, turmeric, and coriander for depth of flavor. Pour in coconut milk and simmer until thickened before stirring in the chickpeas. Serve with rice or naan bread for a complete vegan feast.

These recipes are just a glimpse into how easy it can be to create delicious vegan meals using pantry staples. With these go-to recipes on hand, you'll never be at a loss for what to cook again!

Party Time: Crowd-Pleasing Vegan Appetizers and Finger Foods

Easy Bruschetta Bites

Transform your ordinary party into an extraordinary one with these delectable bruschetta bites. Simply slice a baguette into bite-sized pieces, toast them until golden brown, then top with a flavorful mix of diced tomatoes, garlic, basil, olive oil, and balsamic vinegar. This vibrant appetizer is not only effortless to prepare but also offers a burst of fresh flavors that will leave your guests wanting more.

Crispy Cauliflower Wings

Get ready to impress your friends with these crunchy and irresistible cauliflower wings. Dip florets of cauliflower in a batter made from flour or cornstarch mixed with water or plant-based milk. Then coat each floret in breadcrumbs seasoned with salt and pepper before baking till crispy perfection. Serve alongside vegan ranch dressing or spicy buffalo sauce for the ultimate finger-licking experience.

Mini Veggie Spring Rolls

For an Asian-inspired twist at your next gathering, serve up these delightful mini veggie spring rolls. Fill crisp spring roll wrappers with julienned carrots, bell peppers, cabbage, mushrooms, and bean sprouts seasoned with soy sauce and ginger. Deep fry or bake until golden brown for an appetizer that's packed full of flavor and guaranteed to satisfy everyone's taste buds.

Remember to get creative when it comes to vegan appetizers - there are endless possibilities waiting for you!

On-the-Go Options: Portable Vegan Meals for Busy Lifestyles

When you're always on the move, it can be challenging to find convenient vegan meal options. Luckily, there are several delicious and hassle-free recipes that cater to your busy lifestyle.

1. **Wrap it up**: Wraps are versatile, easy-to-make meals that you can take with you wherever you go. Fill a whole wheat wrap with hummus or avocado spread, fresh vegetables like lettuce, spinach, and tomatoes, and any other toppings of your choice. Roll it up tightly and pack it in a container for a satisfying handheld vegan meal.

2. **Mason jar salads**: Mason jars make excellent containers for prepping healthy salads ahead of time. Layer your favorite veggies in the jar starting with dressing at the bottom followed by sturdier ingredients like cucumbers or carrots first and delicate greens on top. When ready to eat, just give the jar a shake to mix everything together.

3. **Homemade energy bars**: Instead of relying on store-bought granola bars filled with sugar and preservatives, whip up your own batch of homemade energy bars packed with nuts, seeds, dried fruit or even chocolate chips for an added treat. These portable snacks will keep you fueled throughout the day without sacrificing nutrition.

Remember that convenience doesn't mean compromising taste or quality when it comes to vegan meals on-the-go - these options provide both effortless preparation methods and delicious flavors!

Vegan Baking Made Easy: Simple and Delicious Plant-based Treats

Craving something sweet but don't want to spend hours in the kitchen? Look no further than these quick and easy vegan baking recipes.

- **Chocolate Chip Cookies**: With just a few simple substitutions, you can enjoy mouthwatering chocolate chip cookies without any animal products. Swap out butter for vegan margarine or coconut oil, and use flaxseed mixed with water as an egg replacer.

- **Banana Bread**: Overripe bananas are perfect for creating moist and flavorful banana bread. Use applesauce or mashed avocado instead of eggs, and replace dairy milk with almond or soy milk to keep it vegan friendly.

- **Vegan Cupcakes**: Indulge in fluffy cupcakes topped with decadent frosting by swapping out dairy ingredients for plant-based alternatives. Use coconut milk or almond milk instead of cow's milk, and substitute buttercream made from vegetable shortening or non-hydrogenated margarine.

With these simple tweaks, you can create plant-based treats that are just as delicious as their traditional counterparts. Say goodbye to complicated baking methods - try these effortless recipes today!

Seasonal Specials: Vegan Recipes Highlighting Fresh Produce and Festive Flavors

As the seasons change, so do our taste buds. Embrace the vibrant colors and flavors of fresh produce with these vegan recipes that celebrate the bounties of each season. From hearty soups to refreshing salads, you'll find inspiration for every meal.

- **Spring Sensations:** In spring, gardens come alive with a plethora of greens. Try a simple yet satisfying pea and mint soup, where tender peas are blended with fragrant mint leaves for a burst of freshness. Or indulge in a delicate strawberry spinach salad topped with toasted almonds for added crunch.

- **Summer Delights:** Summer is all about light and refreshing dishes. Beat the heat with an irresistible watermelon gazpacho infused with tangy lime juice or savor the sweetness of ripe peaches in a grilled peach salad drizzled with zesty lemon dressing.

- **Autumn Harvests:** As temperatures cool down, warm yourself up with soul-soothing butternut squash soup seasoned generously with cinnamon and nutmeg. Pair it with a kale apple salad tossed in creamy almond butter dressing for layers of textures and flavors.

No matter the season, these recipes will ensure that your vegan meals are bursting with flavor while highlighting nature's delicious offerings effortlessly!

Don't miss out!

Visit the website below and you can sign up to receive emails whenever Tyler Ryan publishes a new book. There's no charge and no obligation.

https://books2read.com/r/B-A-LLJAB-YJUOC

BOOKS 2 READ

Connecting independent readers to independent writers.

Did you love *Vegan Lifestyle for Pregnant Woman*? Then you should read *Monetizing Your Passion: How to Turn Your Hobby into a Lucrative Income Stream*[1] by Tyler Ryan!

[2]

In today's fast-paced world, many people dream of escaping the nine-to-five grind and pursuing their passions full-time. Whether it be painting, playing an instrument, or designing websites, turning a hobby into a lucrative income stream is becoming increasingly attractive. And why not? The idea of making money doing what you love sounds like a dream come true. But how can one actually monetize their passion effectively? In this article, we will delve into the strategies and steps you need to take in order to turn your hobby into a thriving business venture that not only allows you to express your creativity but also pays the bills. So if you're ready to make your dreams become a reality, keep reading as

---

1. https://books2read.com/u/boBxYV

2. https://books2read.com/u/boBxYV

we show you how to unlock the potential within your favorite pastime and transform it into an income-generating machine.

Also by Tyler Ryan

Email Marketing Mastery: A Hands-On Approach for Small Business Owners
Monetizing Your Passion: How to Turn Your Hobby into a Lucrative Income Stream
Vegan Lifestyle for Pregnant Woman